God grant me the Laughter

BY ED F.

CompCare Publishers
Minneapolis, Minnesota

ISBN 0-89638-162-5

Interior design by Maclean & Tuminelly
Cover design by Jerry Gale

Inquiries, orders, and catalog requests should be addressed to:
CompCare Publishers
2415 Annapolis Lane
Minneapolis, Minnesota 55441
Call toll free 800/328-3330
(Minnesota residents 612/559-4800)

1	2	3	4	5
89	90	91	92	93

To John D., my sponsor, my friend

all for one and one for all...

The Three (million)
Alcoholic
       ∨ Musketeers

Why we laugh...

The humor in this book—sometimes gentle, sometimes straight from the shoulder—is for all of us who are recovering from addictions through the principles and fellowship of a Twelve Step Program, especially Alcoholics Anonymous. The author/artist and the contributors all are Twelve Step members.

As recovering people, we know (who knows it better?) that jokes about alcoholics or reeling-drunk comedy routines, intended as casual amusement for the general population, aren't funny. But we, the sober ones, can laugh—because we' re laughing at ourselves, seeing our past behaviors from the wonderful vantage of recovery! Ours is the kind of humor that springs from relief. We count on it to help us stay sober.

Laughter brings perspective. These hearty cartoons by Ed F., who is a recovering alcoholic, are mirrors of ourselves, reflecting with powerful clarity how our drinking or drug-using days contrast with our lives today.

Laughter heals, particularly the laughter that comes when we understand the life-saving difference between "how it was" and "how it is."

And laughter helps us celebrate our recovery. It keeps reminding us of how grateful we are for sobriety—a day at a time—and for the priceless camaraderie of people in the Program.

Thanks to the Twelve Step members who
contributed many of the quips, asides,
recollections, and thoughts in this book,
especially Rick N., Ernie U., and Cecil C.

"Outsiders are sometimes shocked when we burst into merriment over a seemingly tragic experience out of the past. But why shouldn't we laugh? We have recovered, and have been given the power to help others."

—*Alcoholics Anonymous*, AA's classic Big Book

"What I've noticed about AA, and what encouraged me to do this book, is the laughter that greets anyone entering a room getting ready for an AA meeting. If alcoholics have things in common (and I think they do), one of those things is a wonderful sense of humor."

—Ed F.

HOW IT WAS...

From Jack S. at a state roundup:

"Joe H. turned up at his first meeting with serious burns on both ears.

"I asked him how it happened.

"Joe said, 'Well, I was drinking at home one night and my wife was doing the ironing. The phone rang and I answered the iron.'

"I said, 'That explains the burns on your right ear, but what about the left?'

"Joe said, 'The son of a gun called back!' "

Sober Quip:

"Whenever I picked up a bottle, I never knew what else I might pick up!"

From an Al-Anon meeting:

Harry's wife: "Harry always did see things from
a different angle!"

Harry's wife's sponsor: "That comes from pursuing
a drinking career full tilt!"

Thought to live by:

Lean on the Program.

Sober quip:

"When Homer drinks, he sees reality through
   rose-colored glasses."

"ROSÉ-colored, maybe?"

Sober insight:

"Recovery to me means allowing reality back into my
   life—a little at a time.   Reality all at once is
   overwhelming!"

life through the eyes
of a drinking alcoholic...

Thought to live by:

From promises, promises
to priorities, priorities.

Another thought to live by:

First things first.

thanks to Jack Benny

ED F.

Sober exchange:

"So you really believe you were a dolphin in
an earlier life?"

"If I was a dolphin, I was a bottle-nosed dolphin!"

Sober quip:

When the genie in your magic bottle pulls a role
reversal—it's time to put in the cork!

From Harvey Wallbangers to Harvey—in just five years!

Sober recollection:

George A.: "I used to see things when I was drinking!"

Tom W.: "What kinds of things?"

George: "Well, first there was this huge white rabbit... "

Tom: "Yes?"

George: "And then pretty soon there were two huge white rabbits."

Tom: "So when did you decide to join the Program?"

George: "When they started multiplying."

Sober recollection:

"When I couldn't con my real-life friends anymore, I made up some friends I could!"

Sober quip:

"Some guys will go to any lengths to find
  a booze-'em buddy!"

Sober Q and A:

"So who did you drink with?"
"Anybody who happened to be going by
    at the moment!"
    (Caddies and sugar daddies,
    doormen and floormen,
    MBAs and CPAs,
    bikers and hikers,
    bartenders and car-menders,
    couriers and furriers,
    sailors and jailors,
    rookies and bookies,
    movers/shakers and undertakers...

    ...the list goes on...

        and on...

            and on...

                and on!)

Vignette:

Newcomer: "My conscience finally brought me
    to the Program."

Old-timer: "How so?"

Newcomer: "I kept seeing this eyeball staring at me
    from the bottom of my glass! I'm sure it was my
    conscience."

Old-timer: Probably an olive. But never
    mind—whatever works!"

Thought to live by:

Don't wait to laugh until you're entirely happy!

Dr. Jekyll...

Thought to live by:

Pass.
Don't pass out.

Drunk joke for sober people:

An alcoholic wafting down the street on his way home
from the corner pub met two nuns. Since the
sidewalk seemed unusually narrow to him, he found
it hard to move out of their way. So he walked
between them.

Having grown accustomed to seeing double in his
drunken state, he stopped dead, turned around to
stare, and said, amazed, "How did she DO that?"

Sober recollection:

"You might say my whole LIFE was dedicated to the
wine I love."

Thought to live by:

When we put alcohol on an altar,
it's time to alter ourselves!

Sober realization:

"I spent eighteen years building a shrine to Ethyl!"

Al-Anon aside:

"They say the disease of alcoholism is "cunning" and "baffling.""

"So was John when he drank!"

Sober saying:.

HOW: Honest. Open-minded. Willing.

Sober truth:

An alcoholic is an alcoholic is an alcoholic.

Vignette:

"I thought I was too young to be an alcoholic."

"How old are you, son?"

"Nine."

"Well, I thought I was too old to be one!"

"How old are you, sir?"

"Ninety-nine."

Sober recollection:

Old-timer: "I was a card-carrying
   alcoholic—Visa...American Express...Diners'
   Club...Winer's Club...you name it!"

Newcomer, age eighteen: "So was I—a fake ID card!"

Thought to get well by:

The strength of our recovery is in direct proportion
to our ability to laugh at ourselves.

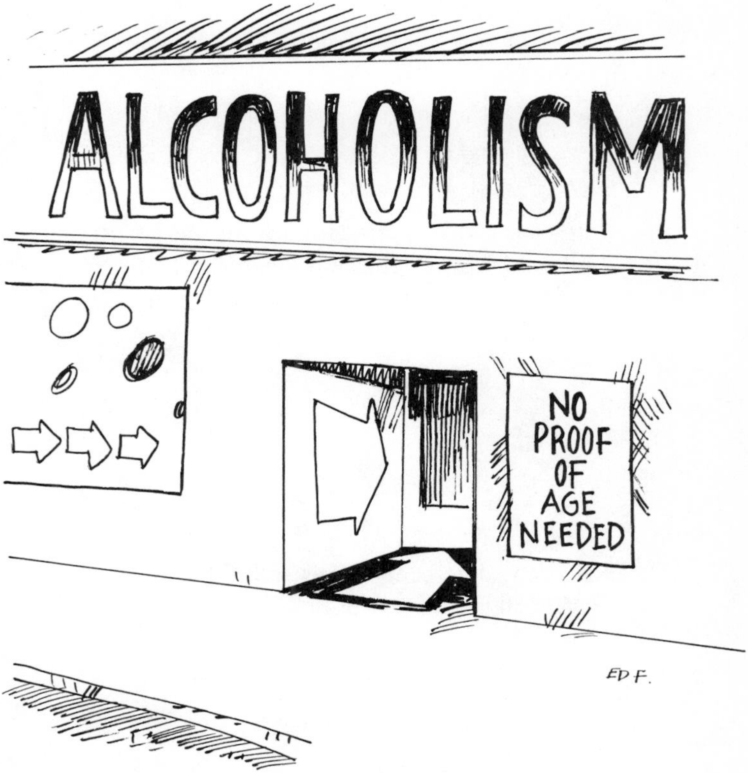
ALCOHOLISM
NO PROOF OF AGE NEEDED
ED F.

Sober summing up by
a twenty-two-year-old recovering junkie:

"Adolescence was no crisis for me—it was a blur!
NOW I'm going through the crisis!"

A straight look back by a former acid rock groupie:

"I wasn't an adolescent—I was an IDOLescent.
With all the wrong idols!"

so my friends
don't want to be
around me anymore

①

who
needs
'em?

②

Sober deduction by a rapelling teen on an aftercare group outing:

"You can't climb rocks stoned!"

when you
take drugs, it's
not you
anymore

ED F.

cocaine...

you
sniff...

it
snuffs...

Sober exchange:

Recovering druggie: "What's it called when you use marijuana all through high school and you DON'T get paranoid or burned out or apathetic?"

Program friend: "Pot luck?"

Recovering druggie: "No. The grace of God."

Thought to live by for teens (and others):

Sometimes the most positive thing
you can say is NO.

"NO, thanks. I don't do that stuff anymore."

"NO, thanks. I've got to be ready for a really big
event: MY LIFE!"

Thought to live by:

From scams and schemes
to honest dreams!

Two Program people, striding past a bar:

"My bucks stopped here."

"My bull STARTED here!"

Current vaudevillia:

"What do you call a YUPPIE who hangs out in a saloon
for years drinking?"

"I don't know. What do you call a YUPPIE who hangs
out in a saloon for years drinking?"

"A DOPA."

"What's a DOPA?"

"A Downwardly mobile, Old, Professional Alcoholic!"

Tip from an inside trader:

Invest in sobriety.
It pays!

Reasons to drink...

1. There's a Republican/Democrat in the White House
2. It was a good day
3. It was a bad day
4. It was a day
5. My wife/husband doesn't understand me
6. My wife/husband understands me too well
7. The little hand is on the '6'
8. Millions are starving in Africa
9. There's a holiday coming up in a few months...

ETC. ETC. ETC.

From a former bar owner, now sober:

"I went from liquid assets to liquid liabilities!"

Alcoholic's escape wish—on a bar trek:

"Jim, Beam me up!"

—Rick N.

an alcoholic's bad dream:

Program note:

"When it comes to helping alcoholics,
 I'd take Bill W. over Sigmund F. any day!"

Sober short story:

"It took years for Walt to come into the Program.
 Before that, he was heavy into analysis. He's the
 only guy I ever knew who could slip on a couch!"

Serious question:

What things matter most in life to an alcoholic?

Serious answer:

1) Alcohol
2) Alcohol
3) Alcohol
4) All of the above

Sober saying:

Alcoholics don't have relationships;
    they take hostages.

Irrational rationale:

"Linda couldn't come to the meeting tonight. She's tied
    up with her research project. It's called 'Exploring
    the Many Angles of Delusion.'"

the love triangle that breaks up marriages:

About Twelve Step people and laughter:

"In laughing at the outlandish behavior of their old
   selves and tipsy others—in tall tales and true
   experiences—they find gratitude, self-forgiveness,
   honesty, and humility."

                                    —Cecil C.

Sober recollection:

"I used to deny being in denial."

Truth for anytime:

Laughter keeps us in touch with ourselves.

you know you're an
alcoholic when...

you know you're an
alcoholic when...

New Years Eve is
the only night of
the year you don't
drink!

you know you're an
alcoholic when...

...your wife tells you
to take out the
garbage, and
she means you

From a recovering chemically dependent writer:

"I went from self-medicating to fabricating—
 unpublishable fantasies.

"It was my 'stream of unconsciousness' period!"

Drunk joke for sober people:

A customer came bounding into a bar and raced up to
 the man who mixed drinks.

The drinker shouted, "Hey, Willie, give me a double
 martini quick before the the fight starts."

The bartender complied, asking, "What fight?"

The customer downed the double and said, "The one
 that's going to start when you find out I don't have
 a cent on me!"

From Cecil C.

Sober observation:

"The Program made an honest woman of me!"

Drunk joke for sober people:

A bartender looked up one morning to see a pink
    elephant, a giant green rat, a purple giraffe, and
    a blue snake.

He stared at the quartet of freaks and then said, "You're
    too early today, fellows. Jim hasn't shown up yet."

From Cecil C.

Sober admission:

"I had an unusually long adolescence! I started doing
    chemicals at fourteen. I went through emotional
    puberty at twenty-eight—when I got sober! Now
    I'm thirty-four and I hope to grow up someday."

Heard at a Twelve Step meeting:

Innovative new member:

"Why not divide the meeting into two groups—one for
  alcoholics with low bottoms, and another for
  alcoholics with high bottoms?"

Ten-year veteran:

"We believe the high bottoms and the low bottoms
  belong together.

"Here, we all wear the same pants!"

Sober hope:

Alcoholism doesn't have to be a bottomless pit—even
  for bottomless drinkers!

Character sketch:

"Dave is a master drunkalog-teller...a low-bottom
  alcoholic who's always playing, 'Can you top this?' "

Just when you think
you've hit bottom...

the bottom drops out...

Twelve Step fact:

The Steps may not be a stairway to paradise, but they
 do give you a way out of the wine cellar!

Drunk joke for sober people:

An alcoholic was undergoing a physical examination.
 When his friendly doctor requested that he hold
 out his arm at full length, he did so. His hand
 shook wildly.

The doctor asked, "Are you still drinking a lot?"

Still shaking, the patient responded, "I've cut 'way
 down. I don't drink a third of what I used to. I spill
 most of it."

From Cecil C.

Truth to recover by:

The Program promises—and delivers—
twenty-four-hour service.

You give it and you get it!

Two words often heard slurred:
"Who, me?"

Sober diagnosis:
"Did you say Albert had DTs?"
"No, but he sure has DDs."
"What are DDs?"
"Delusion and Denial."

Album snapshot:
Recovering old-timer: "I never could see that I had a
    drinking problem. I had horse-blinders on."

Recovering buddy: "Then it couldn't have been too
    tough to learn to say 'Nay!'"

Bottoming out in Manhattan:

"I went from skidding on Park Avenue to parking
on Skid Row."

Sober observation:

Program member, watching a drinking buddy's frequent
assaults on the buffet table for champagne
punch refills:

"Pete always WAS fast with the punch line!"

Definition for today:

"What's a down-and-outer?"

"A problem-drinking executive with too much
down time—he's always *out* to lunch!

Sobering reality:

...AND THE DECISION—BY A BLACKOUT!
(In a showdown with the bottle, the bottle wins.)

ED F.

Signs of sober times in the Alps:

The Saint Bernards have filled their little barrels with Perrier.

Motto to get well by:

Twelve Step help is likely to come from an unlikely source!

Sober memory:

"I would order doubles and see quadruples!"

Nudge toward sobriety:

"When you're seeing 'two for one,' it's time to come
    to the Program."

—Rick N.

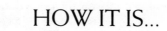

HOW IT IS...

Sobering thought:

Trade those swinging doors for the open door—of AA!

Sober invitation:

The only requirement for membership is the desire
    to stop drinking.

Brief bio from a recovering pro quarterback:

"I went from DTs to TDs!"

Sober promise:

You can replace the shakes with the good vibrations
     of the Program!

Sober reflection:

"I was afraid of being brainwashed in AA.
   After a while my sponsor asked me,
      'Didn't your brain NEED washing?' "

From Ernie U.

Sober truth:

"The First Step is a giant step!"

—*A Day at a Time*

Pinnacles of denial—from hoodwinked spouses—reported by an AA intergroup office:

"One irate woman called the other day and said, 'How long does it take to join your club, anyway? My husband has been trying to get in for months, and he keeps telling me you're full—his name is STILL on the waiting list!' "

"A long-suffering (too long) husband phoned and said, 'Is there any way you can cut your dues? My wife tells me she's been having a hard time saving enough money to join!' "

(Both spouses were set straight!)

Wisdom from Ernie U.:

"The more mistakes we make, the closer we are to doing it right.

"We can actually FAIL our way to success!"

Wisdom from Rick N.:

"We can't even begin to get smart until we know how much we don't know!"

Thought to live by:

Keep it simple:
Don't drink. Read the Big Book. And go to meetings!

Thought to stay sober by from Ernie U.:

"Replace no power with 'NO!' power."

1. We admitted we were powerless over alcohol— that our lives had become unmanageable

2. Came to believe that a power greater than ourselves could restore us to sanity

alcohol brought us to our knees...

...but that's exactly the position we're supposed to bein!

3. Made a decision to turn our will and our lives over to the care of God as we understood Him

4. Made a searching and fearless moral inventory of ourselves

5. Admitted to God, to ourselves and to another human being, the exact nature of our wrongs

6 Were entirely ready to have God remove these defects of character

You can pick them up anytime God

DEFECTS
DEFECTS
DEFECTS
DEFECTS
DEFECTS
DEFECTS

ED F.

7. Humbly asked Him to remove our shortcomings

8. Made a list of all persons we had harmed and became willing to make amends to them all

9 Made direct amends to such people wherever possible except when to do so would injure them or others

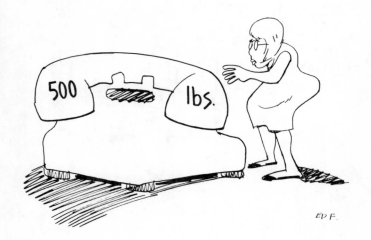

500 lbs.

ED F.

10 continued to take personal inventory and when we were wrong Promptly admitted it

ED F.

11. Sought through prayer and meditation to improve our conscious contact with God as we understood Him, praying only for knowledge of His will for us and the power to carry that out

ED F.

12. Having had a spiritual awakening as a result of these steps, we tried to carry this message to alcoholics and to practice these principles in all our affairs

Sober saying:

"Power through powerlessness."

—A Day at a Time

Sober comparison:

Dependency is lonely.

Recovery is friendly.

Chemical formula:

Alcohol is the universal solvent. It dissolves all sorts of
  things, including marriages, families, friendships,
  careers, bank accounts, human interiors—
  and trust.

Sober saying:

Willingness works wonders.

Sober metaphor:

Recovery is a stairway, not a landing.

Program conversation:

"Where's Horace?"

"He's off Twelve Stepping a Sixth Step defector who's
having trouble facing his defects."

Sober saying:

Easy does it—but do it!

Partial list of "those we had harmed":

> overdrawn banks
> unpaid jewelers
> oil stockbrokers from faraway places
> ex-partners
> fierce saloon-keepers demanding new furniture
> neglected kids, spouses, bosses, parents, dogs,
>   cats, and parakeets.
> long-suffering motel owners
> old gambling buddies waving IOUs
> anyone crazy enough to lend us
>   drinking money
> OURSELVES...

Classic quote:

"Making amends helps us mend."

> —*A Day at a Time*

Sober reality:

"We may need mending AFTER making amends!"

Classic quote:

"May I control my need to control."

—*A Day at a Time*

Sober stopper:

Am I taking myself too seriously?

From a sponsor:

"When you're overdirecting, ask the Producer for help!"

Drunk classic for sober people:

"There was an alcoholic woman in my home town, who, in the course of her drinking, married four times: a millionaire, a magician, a minister, and—finally—an undertaker.

"That's one for the money, two for the show, three to get ready, and four to go!"

From Chico C.

Sober fact:

If we went back to drinking or using, we'd be starting where we left off—at the bottom!

Sobering thought:

We may have another drunk in us—but do we have another recovery?

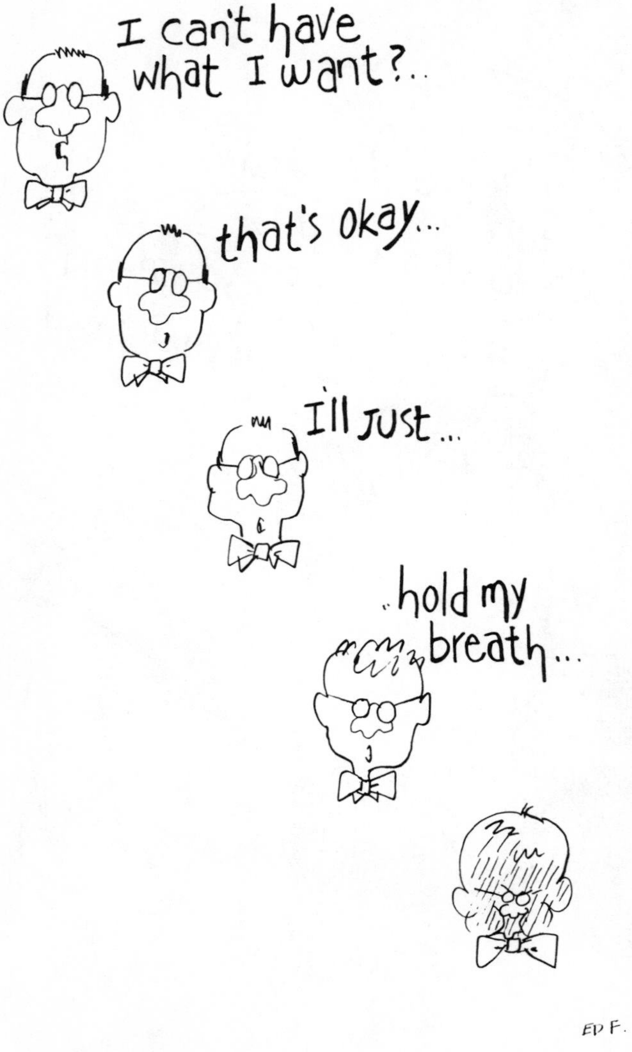
I can't have what I want?...
that's okay...
I'll just...
..hold my breath...
ED F.

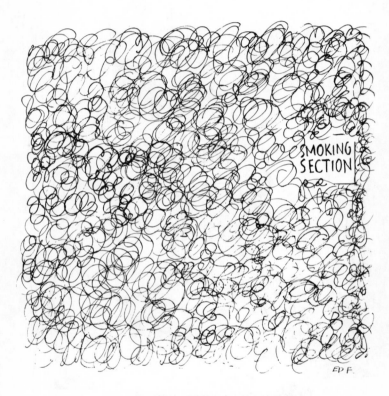

SMOKING
SECTION

ED F.

PICTURE OF AN AA
MEETING IN PROGRESS

Sober reflection:

We have to like ourselves to be able to laugh
at ourselves.

Sober misnomer:

"Who says I was an 'active' drunk?"
I spent half my life out cold on the sofa!"

Sober truth:

"Poor me" can lead to "pour me"—a drink!

Sober reminder about powerlessness:

"Blackouts were regular occurrences in my old drinking
  neighborhood. We had to call on an emergency
  energy source for illumination."

"What kind of energy source?"

"Our Higher Power."

Post-meeting observation:

"When I say 'trespasses,' I really MEAN 'trespasses'!
  I teed off my neighbors by driving my El Camino
  over their putting green!"

Sober counter to a new member's
"who needs a Higher Power anyway?" ploy:

"We never got very far operating under
  our OWN power!"

A Father Martin classic:

"Wherever there are four Irishmen, there's a fifth."

Sober corollary:

Wherever there are two recovering alcoholics,
   there's a meeting.

A new step:

"We used to do the Booze Boogaloo.
   Now we're doing the Java Jive!"

Old recovery ditty:

"I'll take you home again, Caffeine."

Sober definition, for the benefit of a lonely newcomer:

AA is not a dating service or a mating service.

But it IS a friend-finder!

Sober reality:

Spirits never lifted ours.

But a spiritual Program does!

Program exchange:

"They tell us to 'KEEP COMING BACK.' "

"Well, we're sure in the habit! Look at how we 'kept
     coming back' to the corner bar!"

How Some people picture AA...

Tongue twister on the topic of denial (impossible to articulate while drinking):

A drunk sat on a skunk.

The drunk thought the skunk stunk.

The skunk thought the drunk stunk.

Truth was: the drunk AND the skunk stunk.

those telling
drunk-a-
logs
must clean
up
after
meeting

ED F.

Two Program people on their way to Twelve-Step an old drinking buddy:

"Bud says he wants to get his head straight BEFORE he gives up drinking."

"Yup. There goes Bud—putting the cart before the Clydesdale!"

—Rick N.

Sponsorese:

"No more rationalizing, procrastinating, hemming, hedging, fudging, conning, fluffing, or fantasizing. JUST DO IT.

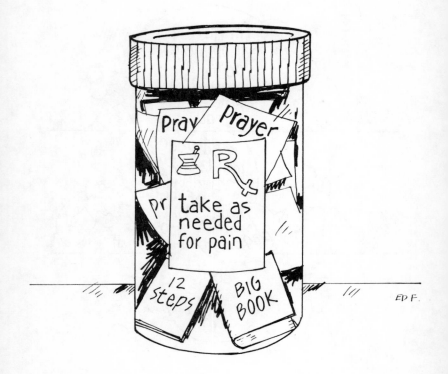

Sober advice:

Never scorn the horn.

Program paradox:

We get it by giving it away!

Corny clarification from Clara S.:

"When we talk about denial, we don't mean
    a river in Egypt!"

Sober truth:

Sponsees help sponsors stay sober too.

Sorry—
I can't go
to the
movies
tonight-
I've been
grounded
by my
sponsor
ED F.

The Twelve Step species, as it has evolved:

honest
open-minded
willing
mutually caring
also with—
    a steel-lined gastrointestinal tract
    resistance to caffeine jitters
    tough lungs and eyes to withstand oxygen
        deprivation and blue haze
        in meeting rooms
    rear cushions, to ward off numbness from
        church basement chairs
    a wild sense of humor
    a propensity for LOUD LAUGHTER!

Sober saying:

Stick with the winners.

Sobering question:

Have I made room for my Higher Power
behind the wheel?

Or in the back seat?

Thought to live by:

Don't keep the faith—spread it around!

AA
So you had a rough drinking career—looks like you've lived a long life...
how old are you?

Newly sober mother, when three kids and one massive sheepdog leap on the bed at 6 A.M.:

"This can't be what they mean by a 'spiritual
   awakening'!"

Sober saying:

"There's nothing that can happen to me today that my
   Higher Power and I—together—can't handle."

Undeniable fact:

"Our worst days sober are better than our best days
   when we were drinking and using."

Sober allusion:

"As James Thurber says, 'Humor is emotional chaos
   remembered in tranquility.' "

Sober saying:

One minute, one hour, one day at a time.

Brief bio:

"Irv was about to be committed for life when he
   decided, instead, to commit himself a day
   at a time— to staying sober!"

the nice thing about
talking to God is you never
have to worry about
getting an answering machine

Program vignette:

Overheard during an Al-Anon meeting: a timber-
quaking, window-rattling SCREAM!

Stunned AA member in the adjacent meeting room:
"What on earth's that?"

Old-timer:
"Oh, just an Al-Anon newcomer's interpretation of
'letting go.'"

Sober saying:

Sometimes we need to protect ourselves from those
who give too much.

ED F.

Sober fact:

Abstinence makes the heart grow fonder.

—Jane N.

Litany of successive compulsions from a member of multiple Twelve Step groups:

"First I was addicted to alcohol...
then prescription drugs...
then nicotine...
then caffeine...
then to my own childhood as a child
    of an alcoholic...
then to gambling...
then to spending...
then to members of the opposite sex....
Altogether that's NINETY-SIX STEPS I'm working!"

Twelve Step transformation:

From under the table
    to willing and able
                   —Rick N.

Sober truism:

There is no chemical solution to a spiritual problem.

Good counsel:

Low Self-ESTEEM?
    Turn to the S TEAM!
    (S stands for sober)!

Codependence to independence—a short script:

HOW IT WAS:

Wait up.

Put on the coffee pot.

Worry that it's all my fault.

Be so relieved when she comes home whole
    that I forget to blow up.

Think of reasons why she drinks

Call her boss in the morning—say she's got a virus
    or the Black (Velvet) Plague

Let my moods reflect hers. (She's mad—I'm mad.
    She's hurt—I'm hurt.)

Feel like dirt.

Feel crazy.

HOW IT IS:

Don't wait up.

Let her put on her own coffee pot.

Realize it's not my fault.

Let her answer when her boss calls.

Stop looking for "reasons why."

Own my own feelings—stop being a mirror
    for hers.

Feel better about myself.

Feel less crazy.

Learn hope from my Al-Anon friends

REDISCOVER HOW TO LAUGH!

Al-Anon aphorism:

As I change myself...
I allow other changes to happen!

A spouse sees the light:

"I went from ENable to UNable:
I realized I couldn't change anybody but me!"

ED F.

Quantum leap—easy does it:

From nine years in hell
 to alive and well!

Sober truth:

Experience is what we get
 when we don't get what we want.

Sober insight:

Recovery is not having to say you're sorry quite so often
 (except when you're working the Ninth Step).

Thought to live by:

Recovery is a path, not a destination.

When I was drinking I was thankful every morning that I was still alive

Now I'm thankful every morning for being ALIVE

Sober summary:

"Sure, I was a practicing alcoholic!

I practiced...

       and practiced...

            and practiced...

                  and practiced...."

Universal recovery feeling, often voiced:

"Help me celebrate the most important day in my life:
my sobriety anniversary!"

Program exchange:

From a puzzled visitor at an open meeting:
"You Program people have had such awful
experiences—you ought to be scarred for life!"

Program host:
"No, just scared for life—about ever going back
to drinking or using!"

HOW SWEET IT IS!

To a non-Program nonbeliever:

'If you really believe recovering addicts are losers,
   just visit an open meeting and hear about
   their victories!"

Program paradox:

Getting help is giving help.
Giving help is getting help.

Twelve Step member to friends:

"One of the greatest things about the Program is:
   I discovered loneliness is treatable!"

Sober comparison:

"What's the difference between a bar buddy
   and a Program pal?"

"A bar buddy cares about alcohol, and a Program pal
   cares about YOU!"

Thought to live by:

We've been in a common bind.
Now we have a common bond!

Another thought to live by:

Laughter cements friendships.

ED F.

Sober truth:

Recovery uncovers...
 buried feelings,
 hidden talents,
 a capacity for love,
 a sense of humor!

    Thought to live by:

   Recovery paves the way to discovery.

Brief bio of a former addict, now a Program speaker:
From hallucinating to elucidating.

Progress (though not perfection):
From cells
 to celebrations—

   from wasting life
    to wanting more of life—

     from down-and-out
      to up-and-at-'em—

        NO WONDER...

...Our cup
runneth
over

Thought to stay sober by:

Every day is a gift.

Unwrap it carefully.

Use it gratefully.

Live it lovingly...

and LAUGH WHEN YOU CAN!

24 hours

ED F.

gift

God grant me the laughter
to help me see the past with perspective,
face the future with hope,
and celebrate today—
without taking myself too seriously.

—Jane N.

God grant me the serenity
to accept the things I cannot change,
courage to change the things I can,
and the wisdom to know the difference.

The Twelve Steps of AA

1. We admitted we were powerless over alcohol—that our lives had become unmanageable.

2. Came to believe that a Power greater than ourselves could restore us to sanity.

3. Made a decision to turn our will and our lives over to the care of God *as we understood Him.*

4. Made a searching and fearless moral inventory of ourselves.

5. Admitted to God, to ourselves, and to another human being the exact nature of our wrongs.

6. Were entirely ready to have God remove these defects of character.

7. Humbly asked Him to remove our shortcomings.

8. Made a list of all persons we had harmed, and became willing to make amends to them all.

9. Made direct amends to such people wherever possible, except when to do so would injure them or others.

10. Continued to take personal inventory, and when we were wrong promptly admitted it.

11. Sought through prayer and meditation to improve our conscious contact with God as *we understood Him,* praying only for knowledge of His will for us and the power to carry that out.

12. Having had a spiritual awakening as the result of these steps, we tried to carry the messsage to other alcoholics and to practice these principles in all our affairs.

The Twelve Steps and Twelve Traditions of AA reprinted with permission of AA World Services, Inc.

The Twelve Traditions of AA

1. Our common welfare should come first; personal recovery depends on AA unity.

2. For our group purpose there is but one ultimate authority— a loving God as He may express Himself in our group conscience. Our leaders are but trusted servants; they do not govern.

3. The only requirement for AA membership is a desire to stop drinking.

4. Each group should be autonomous except in matters affecting other groups or AA as a whole.

5. Each group has but one primary purpose—to carry its message to the alcoholic who still suffers.

6. An AA group ought never endorse, finance, or lend the AA name to any related facility or outside enterprise, lest problems of money, property and prestige divert us from our primary purpose.

7. Every AA group ought to be fully self-supporting, declining outside contributions.

8. Alcoholics Anonymous should remain forever nonprofessional, but our service centers may employ special workers.

9. AA, as such, ought never be organized, but we may create service boards or committees directly responsible to those they serve.

10. Alcoholics Anonymous has no opinion on outside issues; hence the AA name ought never be drawn into public controversy.

11. Our public relations policy is based on attraction rather than promotion; we need always maintain personal anonymity at the level of press, radio, and films.

12. Anonymity is the spiritual foundation of all our traditions, ever reminding us to place principles before personalities.